When I Grow Up

True-Story Devotions of Children
Once Destined for Poverty,
Now Transformed by Hope

Coni Knepper

Photographs by
Christina Whittaker

All scriptures were taken from the English Standard
Version of the Bible unless otherwise noted.

The proceeds from *When I Grow Up* will go to support
Hope of the Nations Primary School.

f3ISBN: 1545218390
ISBN-13: 978-1545218396

FOREWORD

I recently heard a pastor of a large church say to his congregation, "I am a sixty-year-old youth minister." He then went on to describe that his major focus through the years and still today is ministering to children. He spoke about how he believes youth ministry is the most fruitful and fulfilling ministry over the long haul. Many studies show that the highest rate of conversion and lasting impact comes from teaching children the truth of God's Word. It is smart and biblical to "start children off on the way they should go, and even when they are old they will not turn from it" (Prov. 22:6 New International Version). The ripple effect is powerful for generations yet unborn and has the potential of changing an entire community!

I have had the joy of knowing Coni and her husband, Harold, for more than forty years. When she was a high-school student, Coni started coming to the church where I was a pastor. She was loved by the church family, she gave her life to Jesus, she sang in our church choir, and God grew in her a passion to touch other young people with his love, which she and Harold did for a number of years as our youth ministers.

In their more than fourteen years of ministry in Tanzania,

they have touched the lives of thousands of children and young people and have seen them transformed by God's love and given them a bright future to the glory of God.

In this remarkable book, you will discover a unique fourteen-day devotional journey that will take your family on a marvelous adventure. You will learn about the lives of children from Tanzania, East Africa. Your family will feel as if they have been to Kamala village together while learning to appreciate missions overseas. In every chapter, you will read a real-life story of a child once destined for pain and poverty but now living out God's plan for his or her life. It is down-to-earth, practical, and life changing.

The book focuses on Godly characteristics—such as grace, joy, forgiveness, and ten others—using key verses from the Bible. There are thought-provoking questions at the end of each chapter for discussion and application. You will love the full-color pictures from Tanzania, but most of all the pictures of the children whose stories are told.

The stories are easy enough for your children to read, and the discussion questions will challenge your spiritual journey as well as theirs. The raw stories about children in Tanzania will capture the heart of your family, so get ready for some changes. They will move your children to do something for others and to appreciate what they have. This devotional is not like any other. When I Grow Up can also be used for home school, Sunday school classes, and other discussion groups.

I had no idea forty years ago, when I first met Coni, how God was going to use her, but I knew he was up to something big in her life. When I read her book for the first time, I had to wipe away some tears—tears that came because I know Coni and because I realize the God that is changing the lives of children through her is the same God that changed her life years ago when she was a teenager. People came around her and loved her to the Lord, just like she is now doing in Tanzania. I love the stories and the sense of genuineness, realism, and down-to-earth nature of what is shared. The issues she deals with are everyday issues for everyone but are multiplied many times over in Tanzania because of the poverty, cultural and family dysfunctions, and spiritual darkness.

My prayer is that God will use this book to ignite a fire within you to help touch the lives of children of your world in fresh ways so that you will become a beacon of hope for your family, church, community, and beyond, to the glory of God!

Bryce Jessup
President Emeritus
William Jessup University

ACKNOWLEDGMENTS

Without Hope of the Nations Primary School, there would be no book. Without Geanie Eaton and Mary Freer, there would be no school. These two women are saints! God stirred in their hearts to start a school in Tanzania in 2006. They collected over seven thousand books and sent two containers full of supplies. Both women have visited the school over nine times. They have taught teachers seminars and helped set up the school offices. Thank you, from the children and staff of Hope of the Nations.

There are many people who contributed to finalizing When I Grow Up. I am immensely thankful.

Thank you, Stan Faddis. Through your love for Hope of the Nations, God used you to start the first edit and point me in the right direction for publishing.

Many mornings, Donna Garcia and I read each chapter over and over. We laughed and cried together. Thank you, Donna, for your expertise as an author and editor.

When my book had no pictures or illustrations, God knew I needed a professional photographer. Christina Whittaker, you captured what was in my heart. Thank you also for putting the book together. It would still be on my laptop if not for your work.

To the many friends and family, thank you for taking

the time to read the first drafts. And to the man who is my spiritual dad, Bryce Jessup, your encouragement over the years has given me boldness to even try to write a book.

Saving the best for last, thank you to my husband, Harold. I have loved and been deeply loved by you for over forty-two years. Thank you for listening to me ramble on about a book I wanted to write. The stories in When I Grow Up wouldn't be real if God had not called us to Tanzania.

Thank You, Father God, for the call.

In Him,
Coni Knepper

TABLE OF CONTENTS

Fun Facts..1

Hope..8

Forgiveness Part 1....................................14

Forgiveness   Part   2................................19

Prayer..25

Mercy...32

Patience...37

Joyfulness..42

Love Part 1..47

Love Part 2..49

Thankfulness...53

Peace...58

Acceptance..62

Grace...68

About the Author.....................................74

About Hope of the Nations Ministries..........76

FUN FACTS

Learn why 👫 in Kamala village love to eat termite bugs. Or imagine 🏊 with 🐟 in the longest lake in the world.

Read why 👴 live in one-room 🏠 with their entire family.

These are just a few fun facts about the life in Kamala village, in 🌍 .

Follow the picture words and you will discover how some of your culture matches the way 👫 in Kamala village live.

🏞 Tanganyika is 410 miles long, up to 45 miles wide, and almost 1 mile deep. It holds 16 percent of the world's fresh water and provides jobs, food, and 💧 water for four different countries bordering its shores.

Burundi, Congo, Zambia and Tanzania all benefit from the vastness of 🏞 Tanganyika.

Over 250 species of cichlid 🐟 and 80 other kinds of 🐟 live in the beautiful turquoise colored waters. There are no 🏭 along the shores to pollute it. If you visit your neighborhood pet store, you might find 🐟 from

1

Tanganyika.

Because ___ is the primary source of ___, it is common for men to make small ___ from ___ found along the lake. They carve the ___ out by hand. Every night, you can see hundreds of ___ on the lake with glowing ___ . Some nights, it looks like there is a city on the lake, but really, it is the lights from the ___ all lined up.

Seven thousand people live in the tropical Kamala village. The weather is much like Hawaii. It ___ six months out of the year and doesn't ___ the other six months. Because Tanzania is only five hundred miles from the equator day and night are each twelve hours long. There is no daylight savings time.

The closest big town is Kigoma, a forty-five minute ___ from Kamala. Walking through Kamala village you see homes made of mud and sticks, mamas cooking on ___, and children helping to carry buckets of water from the lake.

A family might have seven to nine ___ in a one-room ___ . Out of respect for ___ , it is common to have ___ living with the family too.

During ___ season you might see a group of ___ chasing flying termites. They make for a great snack.

2

The termites come up from the muddy ground after a hard ☁️. They are easy to catch and taste like a nut. People also roast them over the 🔥 when serving them for a meal.

The 🧍 do not have toys like 🧍 have in the USA. They play outside with things they make out of 🪓 and plastic bags. Girls are usually busy with gathering 🪵 for 🔥 to cook on, fetching buckets of 💧 and taking care of younger siblings.

Swahili is the language spoken in Tanzania. Even so, English is the second language people speak. Typically, those in leadership in the country speak English. The disadvantage is English is only taught to students who have the opportunity to attend high school or college.

Hope of the Nations Primary School is the only school teaching students how to read, write and speak English beginning in Kindergarten and continuing up through the seventh grade. Hope of the Nations Primary School provides a quality education for 225 🧍 who would not be able to go to school without help. With a quality education, 🧍 can pass the required marks on the National exam and be chosen to attend high school for free. These students will grow up and become leaders in their communities.

While attending Hope of the Nations Primary School, students receive two hot meals each day. For breakfast, the eat uji. It looks like cream of wheat, but made with ground coconut shells, small , flour, and different . Then, it is boiled until it is soft. The LOVE it! School lunch and beans with spinach, and chapati. Sweets and desserts are not something you find in Kamala.

In their daily life, there is no such thing as lunchtime, only tea in the morning and a late night meal. The most common food eaten is made of flour and water. It is called ugali. It looks like , but with no flavor and it is sticky. Eating ugali takes practice. First, you take a handful, roll it up in your hand and then dip it into some sauce. Small and spinach made with tomatoes and garlic are the favorite kinds of sauces the children enjoy.

Go to my website for FREE downloadable resources.
www.coniknepper.com

X X X X X X X X X

Now that you have learned some fun facts about the children that live in Kamala, this will help you better understand and enjoy their culture. At the beginning of every story, there are Bible verses to read together and a different Godly character trait highlighted. There are discussion questions at the end of each story. These are to stretch you spiritually.

Enjoy and have fun!

FUN FACTS
Discussion Questions

1. Compare how you live with how the children live in Kamala village. Most of the world's children live like the families in Kamala.

2. What are some interesting facts you learned about Lake Tanganyika?

3. What was the name of the breakfast food the children love? What is your favorite food?

4. The children in Kamala eat one meal a day at home. How would it feel to only eat once a day?

5. As a family, agree to only eat one small meal a day for two days. Then discuss how you felt.

6. The children in Kamala are happy to play with sticks and stones. For one day, put away your toys and phones. Then discuss how life was different.

HOPE

Rejoice in hope, be patient in tribulation, be constant in prayer.

Romans 12:12

Joseph is a seven-year-old bundle of energy. He is full of mischievous acts and lives in a little mud hut made of sticks.

Joseph has always been up to something. Like the time he let all the air out of my tires! This used to be his way of welcoming new people to the neighborhood, or he would use a key to scratch your car. If something went missing from your vehicle, you could be sure Joseph had something to do with it.

Before Joseph was five, both his parents passed away. Since then, his aunt has raised him, but she has only a few resources to provide food and clothing. With a smile on his face daily, Joseph looked for food in the village garbage or stole from tourists. Besides food, what he really wanted was to go to school. Next door to Joseph's little mud hut is a public school for children his age. There are 1,700 students and 22 teachers in grades K-7. The public school requires students to wear new black shoes and uniforms. Students also have to bring jugs of water and brooms to help clean the school.

Obviously, Joseph could not afford to attend public school. He never gave up hope. As Joseph watched other children walk to school, one day, it would be his turn. He would go to school even though he had no one to help him.

Weekly, Joseph would try and sneak onto the Hope of the Nations Primary School campus. Every time he heard the same thing,

"You have to be five years old." This is the age at which the government allows students to begin.

The day finally came when his aunt told him, "You look like a five-year-old, and you want to go to school, so you must be five." With no parents or a birth certificate, no one was sure of his age.

Then came registration day at Hope of the Nations Primary School. Joseph was the first child to arrive, and the smallest person in line, but he had the biggest smile! This time, he was sure the school would say YES. His hopes were high. Waiting in line with the other students, he jumped up and down with excitement. With Joseph's financial situation, there would be no school fees to pay. The school would provide new shoes, a uniform, books, supplies, and two hot meals a day.

These meals would be more food than Joseph had ever eaten in one day. This would also mean no more searching for food.

Joseph got into Hope of the Nations Primary School that

day. He received new uniforms, shoes, a Bible, a notebook, crayons, and pencils! If you come to school at lunchtime, you will see Joseph gobbling down LOTS of good food.

He is now in the fourth grade and at the top of his class. He can speak English so well that he helps translate for visitors that come to tour the school. Instead of stealing, he is learning Godly characteristics. Stealing, letting the air out of tires and keying cars is not what Joseph thinks about anymore. Now he has hope. When he grows up, he dreams of becoming a doctor to bring medical help to his community.

In his village, there are no doctors. People die every day from diseases like malaria, HIV, and cholera. We, at Hope of the Nations, believe that with the continued help from God, Joseph will one day become a doctor.

HOPE
Discussion Questions

1. Is there anything in Joseph's life that is like your life? Have you ever been mischievous?

2. Why do you think Joseph wanted to go to school?

3. What do you appreciate about getting an education?

4. When Joseph was waiting in line for registration, what do you think was going through his mind? How do you think he felt?

5. Have you ever wanted something that you were willing to wait for?

6. Joseph hoped for an education and food. What are your hopes and dreams?

7. Do you think the hopes and dreams you have are ones that God has for you or ones that you want for yourself? How do you know?

Just for Fun

Raise your right hand straight up over your head. Point to the ceiling.

Reach your right hand over your head. Can you reach your left ear?

If you can you are old enough to start school in Tanzania.

This is the technique people had to use for years because children did not have birth certificates.

FORGIVENESS
Part 1

*Put on then as God's chosen ones, holy and beloved,
compassionate hearts, kindness, humility, meekness, and
patience, bearing with one another, and if one has a complaint
against another, forgiving each other; as the Lord has forgiven
you, so you must also forgive. And above all these put on love,
which binds everything together in perfect harmony.*

Colossians 3:12-14

David and Maria are brother and sister who are twins.
When we found them Maria was shy and quiet. David was an
outspoken angry little boy.

Every Friday in Kamala village, Hope of the Nations
Primary School has a Kids Club. It is a place where children
come from all over the neighborhood to play games, eat
snacks, and hear about Jesus.

One Friday, a set of twins came to Club. Their clothes
were covered in dirt and stomachs protruding. The little
boy was very sick and looked like he might not even live
another day. His sister hunched over, with eyes circled in
darkness. Both were hungry and wore ragged clothes.

I could not help but take them into my arms.

Immediately, the Kids Club leaders grabbed them from me and took them to the hospital. I had to do something. I was on a mission. I decided to go door to door, asking everyone if they knew these children.

The population in Kamala village is 7,000 people, 3,000 of them are children. Many of the children are without parents. I didn't know if this set of twins had parents alive. But I knew there had to be someone who recognized them. After talking to the neighbors, I found out their names, David and Maria. Their mother passed away from HIV several months before, and there was no sign of a father.

Since that time, David had been living on the streets, eating garbage. A neighbor took Maria in as her house girl to care for younger children and clean the house. Both David and Maria looked to be about four years old. Later I found out they were six years of age.

My temper flared! How dare these people take advantage of this little girl? How could they leave David to survive on his own?

Both children were at the Mercy House for several weeks receiving care and medicine. When they were well enough, they started school at Hope of the Nations Primary School.

David got into fights every day. In Kindergarten, he poked his eye with a pencil and blinded himself. Maria kept to herself because she had no friends. Both seemed to be learning their subjects, but I knew they were very bitter inside.

The hurt and pain they had suffered needed forgiveness. I also had to forgive. I met with David and Maria and shared how we must forgive others because Jesus forgives us. Not forgiving those who have hurt us makes us sad and angry. Forgiveness is for our FREEDOM, not necessarily for the other person.

David shared how he did not want to be mad at everyone. He prayed and forgave the people who had harmed him. Maria asked if she would have to go live with the people again if she forgave them. With tears in my eyes, I said, "No, forgiveness is letting go of the pain and letting God deal with them." She prayed and forgave the family that had hurt her.

Mama Joy, a woman who works at Hope of the Nations, asked if David and Maria could live with her and her two children. The twins have now lived with Mama Joy for more than ten years. They are a part of a family that follows Jesus. David had eye surgery and can now see again. He makes people laugh wherever he goes. David is full of joy and happiness. Maria has grown into a sweet young girl who loves Jesus, and she has many friends. They both have chosen to forgive the people that mistreated them. I, too, have forgiven the families who wronged these precious children.

A few years ago, their grandmother came to school. They had never met her. She is their mother's mom. She heard about her grandchildren living under the care of Hope of the Nations. She wanted to come to see her grandchildren and say thank you.

The children still see their grandmother from time to time.

For some time, Maria would not say what she wanted to be when she grows up. Why do you think this happened?

Once she forgave people, she realized she would like to work at the Hope of the Nations Training Center. Maybe she will be a seamstress and make wedding gowns.

David wants to be a pastor and teach people about grace and forgiveness. We are sure that God will use these twins to change their world.

This makes me wonder: What could happen to your world if you forgive others?

FORGIVENESS PART 1
Discussion Questions

1. Who benefits from forgiveness?

2. What did Maria and David do to forgive others?

3. How did not forgiving others cause David and Maria to act?

4. How do you think Maria and David felt after they forgave people?

5. Are there people you need to forgive? Who are they?

6. The other side of forgiveness is confessing what you've done wrong. Are there people you need to apologize to? Who are they?

7. How do you think you would feel if you forgave the people who hurt you?

8. Make a plan to talk with the people you need to forgive and apologize to.

FORGIVENESS
Part 2

If we confess our sins, he is faithful and just to forgive us our sins, and to cleanse us from all unrighteousness.

1 John 1:9

Harriet is a smart and curious little girl. She loves to learn and to read.

Harriet's mother and father are on staff with Hope of the Nations Primary School. Her parents are nationals (people born in Tanzania) who love their country. The family follows Jesus Christ as their savior. Her mother is the kindergarten teacher, and she has been teaching Harriet to speak and read in English from the time Harriet was small. Learning English at a young age has given Harriet an advantage at school.

When Harriet was in the second grade, a life-changing event was about to happen in a way no one could have imagined.

It was a typical sunny day at school. Bible memory verses and Bible stories were part of a daily routine. Harriet was at the top of her class in Bible and most other subjects. Harriet's Bible teacher noticed she was talking while he was trying to explain the story.

The school rules were clear that a teacher was to send a child to the office if she or he was being disrespectful. It seemed Harriet was not going to listen to the story.

The Bible teacher became frustrated. He decided that he would have her sit in her mother's kindergarten class instead of the office. He thought her mother could make her listen. Harriet and the teacher walked briskly toward the kindergarten class. The teacher was pulling Harriet by her arm. Harriet's mother met face to face with the teacher. They spoke harsh words to each other.

After much discussion, the teacher decided he would take Harriet back to class. She would miss the next recess instead of going to the office. But the big problem was that he was angry. He stormed back to the classroom with Harriet in tow. As he was shutting the classroom door behind him, he did not notice Harriet's finger was in the door. He slammed the door and cut off the first joint of her middle finger. Harriet screamed in pain. When he heard the scream, the teacher reopened the door. The whole class raced to see what had happened! Meanwhile, Harriet's mother had gone back into the kindergarten classroom. She was unaware that anything had happened to her daughter.

Hope of the Nations is not proud of what happened this day at school. Complete chaos took over. Children from all the classes were crying, teachers were yelling, and Harriet's mother was trying to get Harriet to the doctor. The nearest hospital is in Kigoma, which is a twenty-minute drive from Kamala village or an hour brisk walk. In Kamala there are clinics; however they are only able to give basic first aid. An injury of this kind could not be taken care of in Kamala.

Harriet's father, my husband, and I were all out of town. Harriet's mother called another staff member to help her. She grabbed the cut-off part of the finger, put it in a plastic bag, and hurried off to the clinic.

After several hours, the doctors at the clinic admitted they could not sew the finger back on. They bandaged her little finger and sent Harriet home.

When I returned from out of town some weeks later and finally saw her finger, it broke my heart. I realized Harriet would have to look at a stump at the end of her finger for the rest of her life.

She would know that her Bible teacher had cut it off.

It was an accident, but one done in anger.

The Bible teacher never came to visit Harriet, nor did he ever apologize, which left me no choice but to let him go. None of us will ever forget this sad time at our school. I did not know if we could recover from all the hurt and anger.

Then God changed everything. It started with one little girl's act of forgiveness.

Harriet had been praying that her finger would grow back. She hoped the teacher would know that she had forgiven him, even if he never asked for forgiveness. Every day for weeks, she had to go and get the bandage replaced with a clean one. Then one day, as the doctor was unwrapping the bandage, he noticed something. There was a fingernail. A nail bed was starting to grow out of the stump. Every day, the doctor could see more and more of the nail and the tip of Harriet's finger growing back. What was impossible for man to understand, God could do.

Today, Harriet is in the sixth grade. She has not only forgiven the teacher, but she also apologized for her behavior in class. Her finger has grown back completely. It has full movement and feeling. It is a miracle.

The bigger miracle is that Harriet and her family were able to forgive the hurt that happened to them. The teacher no longer works at the school. He was unwilling to take any responsibility for the accident. Everyone at Hope of the Nations is praying that one day he will accept Harriet's forgiveness and understand what anger can do to a person's choices.

When Harriet grows up, she wants to be a doctor and learn more about helping sick people. Or she would like to be a teacher like her mother. Harriet will never forget the time God healed her completely, not only her finger but also her heart.

FORGIVENESS PART 2
Discussion Questions

1. Have you ever been disobedient to a teacher or to your parents? When? What happened?

2. When Harriet got hurt, whose fault do you think it was? Why?

3. Is there ever a time it is OK to be angry? When? Why?

4. What is the miracle in this story?

5. If you could say anything to the teacher in this story, what would it be?

6. From God's word, what do you think Jesus is saying to the teacher?

7. From the previous story and questions, how is your forgiveness plan going?

8. Share with your family who you have forgiven and why?

9. Have you gone and ask forgiveness from someone you might have hurt?

PRAYER

Therefore, confess your sins to one another, and pray one for another, that you may be healed. The prayer of a righteous person has great power as it is working.

James 5:16-17

Godfrey is an intelligent orphaned boy who has a strong desire to please God in all he does. He is a prayer warrior.

The fifth-grade class decided stealing, from a supply closet at school would be a fun idea. They not only took things but destroyed papers and extra curriculum. Even their favorite games had pieces missing.

I found the closet while checking on some other books I was looking for. I felt my heart race, anger, and disappointment were building up inside me. I could not believe the class would steal and destroy their classroom supplies. At the time, they were our oldest students. They had been at the school the longest. I was especially shocked that Godfrey would do such a thing. It made me think - Was our school even making a difference?

After calming down, I asked, "What made you think stealing and destroying would be a good idea?" Their response was even more shocking. No one said a word, only disrespectful glares, and silence filled the room. Except for Godfrey, he sat with his head down on his desk. During lunchtime, you could see him praying instead of eating. He did not hang out with the rest of his classmates.

I called for a guardian, teachers, and fifth-grade meeting in the hope of finding out why this happened. The parents' response was no better than that of the children. They said, "Why didn't you lock the closet?"

Pointing his finger at the students, a parent said, "How can you expect these children to not steal?" Another idea they came up with was to have a punishment room. Hope of the Nations Primary School does not and will NEVER spank children as punishment. Yet the adults thought this would be the right way for the children to learn. Beating at school is what they had grown up with.

Godfrey sat by himself with his head down, crying while the other students stared out the window.

After the meeting, all the 5th-grade class went home for one week to think about what they had done. The students were to return with their own supplies such as paper, pens, and exercise books. Parents were not happy about this decision. Godfrey had no parents to go home to. His grandmother raises him because his parents abandoned him when he was two years old. I kept thinking about whether the school was making a difference in the children's lives. Godfrey was the only student that showed any kind of remorse. He seemed to be struggling to tell me something.

Over the next week, many parents and guardians came to my office with all kinds of advice.

Godfrey's grandmother said she could not believe Godfrey would be a part of all this. The parents and guardians thought I should get locks for the closet door and move on. In other words, let their child come back to school with no consequences or expectations of proper behavior. My heart sank, as these were parents that I thought had more respect for the school, and for their children.

I went home and prayed for an answer. "Please Lord, soften the hearts of these children to know who you are." Their week of no school had ended, with still no remorse insight.

Later that day, while I was teaching in the third grade English class. I noticed the fifth graders were sitting outside my room. Glancing outside, I asked what they were doing. "Waiting for you, Mama Joshua," they replied. I said, "I still have sixty minutes of my class left to teach." They walked away with their heads down. Whispering out the window to them, I said, "You can come back when I'm finished." With a skip in their step, they went back to their classroom. Hope filled my heart. It was a long hour.

While putting my books away, all twenty of the fifth graders walked into my classroom. I sat in a chair in front of the class. Godfrey led the students in placing individual letters in my lap. Quietly they sat down, waiting for my response.

My lips quivered as I read the first words; there was no way to hold the emotions back. I cried through every letter. Each one was personally written from the heart. I asked if anyone had told them to write these apologies. "No, we wrote them ourselves."

The letters were full of repentance. They admitted what they had done and begged for forgiveness. They could not keep living with the lies and unforgiveness in their hearts. Each had different scriptures to share.

The children then came and sat on the floor surrounding me. We all hugged and wept together. After a few minutes, Maria stood up and said, "My heart feels free! Just like you have taught us. When we are honest and say, we are sorry, there is freedom!" Godfrey smiled as his classmates cheered.

Godfrey's letter was full of apology for his class, yet he had not stolen anything. Since the incident, he had been praying that I would be able to forgive them and that God would use him to help his classmates tell the truth. I knew they were capable of apologizing, and I knew they understood what they had done.

Godfrey's class will never be the same. They will always remember what forgiveness feels like, and so will I.

Since then, I have shared their letters with staff, parents, and guardians. With looks of shock on their faces, the parents could not believe what they read. "Someone told them to write these," one parent said. "Yet, each one is different," I said. There was no arguing that they wrote the words themselves, from hearts wanting to be right with God. Hope of the Nations Primary School is not perfect, but it is making a difference.

Godfrey wants to be an artist and a pastor when he grows up. He is a born leader and prayer warrior. He knows God will never leave him and hears his prayers.

PRAYER
Discussion Questions

1. Godfrey did not steal anything from the school. What did he do?

2. Have you ever prayed for someone? Who? What happened?

3. What happened after Godfrey prayed for his class?

4. There is power in praying for others. Ask God for whom you need to pray for. Then make a list of the people that come to mind.

5. Is there a friend at school that is not behaving well? Maybe they need prayer and a friend.

6. Is there someone in your life who makes you mad? Pray for them so you can forgive them. Ask God if you need to change.

7. Pray for the people in your life that do not know Jesus Christ as their Savior. Then wait and see how God answers your prayers.

Prayer Journals are a fun way to keep track
of answered prayers.
You can find your free prayer journal pages in
the folder you downloaded from my site.
Each page includes a different theme to help
you remember people and places to pray about.

MERCY

Blessed be the God and Father of our Lord Jesus Christ, the Father of mercies, and the God of all comfort, who comforts us in all our affliction, so that we may be able to comfort those who are in affliction, with the comfort with which we ourselves are comforted by God.

2 Corinthians 1:3-4

Shida is a shy little girl whose life started as a miracle. Her mother did not want her, but she was born anyway. As soon as Shida could walk, she played outside all day to fend for herself. Daily, she walked to the Hope of the Nations Primary School, located next door to her mud hut.

At age five, Shida started Kindergarten at Hope of the Nations School. When she was in second grade, her teacher noticed she was losing weight and not feeling well. After visiting with the school nurse, they found out that she was very sick.

Shida's Father was eighty years old and had twenty-four children. Shida was number twenty-two; she had two younger sisters to watch after. In Tanzania, it is common for older sisters to care for the younger ones. Even while Shida was in school and not feeling well, she came home from school and cooked for her younger siblings.

Hope of the Nations Primary School teachers often went door to door in the neighborhood. They visited families and shared the gospel. One day Shida decided to go with them. They were going to visit the home of a sick woman and her family. Shida had always been shy and not very talkative. That day was very different. As the group sat down with the woman, Shida started sharing how much she loved Jesus. She shared that God was her Father and that she knew Jesus Christ died for her sins. The teachers watched in amazement. Here was a little girl who had never spoken about her faith to anyone. Right then, the woman prayed with a five-year-old to receive Christ as her Savior.

Shida would go on to be used by God. She shares the love of Jesus wherever she goes.

Unfortunately, Shida's health continued to decline. Hope of the Nations has a home called Mercy House, where nurse Eva lives and works. People come to receive free medical care. The school decided to have Shida admitted into the Mercy House to get the attention she needed. Eva agreed to take Shida until her health improved enough to attend school again. Three weeks went by, and still, Shida had not come back to school.

I asked Eva about Shida; she said, "Actually Shida is well, but my husband and I are enjoying having her with us." Eva and her husband had not been able to have children of their own. I asked her if she wanted Shida as her daughter? As the words came out of my mouth, I thought, "What am I saying?" Eva almost jumped out of her shoes with excitement! She said, "YES, we would love to adopt Shida if that would be possible." Eva felt great compassion and mercy toward Shida.

After meeting with Shida's Father, he agreed because he could not care for his 24 children. They were all crowded into a two-room home, and food was scarce. Eva and her husband would keep Shida.

From that day until now, Shida has a mommy and a daddy that love her, and she loves them. We changed her name to Rose because, in Swahili, Shida means a problem. Rose was an answer to Eva's prayers. She is never a problem, but a sweet girl full of mercy and love.

Rose is now in good health. She graduated from Hope of the Nations Primary School and is attending a top school in Tanzania.

When Rose grows up, she wants to be like her mommy, helping sick people at the Mercy House. She also loves telling people about Jesus.

MERCY
Discussion Questions

1. What does mercy mean?

2. What is the difference between mercy and grace?

3. Who showed mercy to Shida?

4. Has anyone ever showed you mercy? Who? When?

5. Have you ever shown mercy to someone? Who? When?

6. Do you know Jesus Christ died for your sins?

7. Have you ever given your life to Jesus? When?

8. Remember how Shida shared Jesus with the sick woman. Have you ever shared what Jesus has done for you?

9. Write out how you would share Jesus with someone. Then share it with a family member. Pray and ask God to help you. He will!

Need help on how to share the Good News with friends and family?
Find your FREE journal page in your downloaded folder. The pages are fun and easy to understand.

PATIENCE

And we urge you, brothers, admonish the idle, encourage the fainthearted, help the weak, be patient with them all. See that no one repays anyone evil for evil, but always seeks to do good to one another and to everyone. Rejoice always.

I Thessalonians 5:14-16

Yo-Yo is a boy with a huge heart. He is full of energy, and the only educated person in his family.

I was present when Yo-Yo was born. His birth name is Angel. From day one, he has been an energetic boy. The name Yo-Yo comes from Kids Club. At clubs, the teachers say, "Watoto," in a booming voice. Watoto means "children" in Swahili. The children answer with Yeahhhh in their loudest voice. When Yo-Yo was very young, he would go to the kids club and answer, "Yo-Yo" instead of Yeahhhh. From then on, Yo-Yo stuck as his name.

Yo-Yo is the third of four children. His older sisters have never gotten the chance to go to school. Hope of the Nations Primary School first opened after his sisters were not living at home.

His parents do not have full- time jobs. There are days when his mom walks through the village, looking for food to feed her family of six. His father sometimes finds day jobs helping to build brick buildings in the town.

When I first meet Yo-Yo's mother, she was making homebrew, which is illegal alcohol. It was the only job she could find. But, after surrendering her life to Jesus. She showed interest in attending Hope of the Nations Jewelry Making School. It didn't take long until Yo-Yo; his mom and siblings were all making jewelry. Even his dad was creative in making necklaces. They sold many beautiful pieces in the Hope of the Nations store.

Other mamas and their children have been able to make jewelry and sell it for food. The families also sell their wares in Kigoma town to tourists. Sometimes it is hard to be patient waiting for people to buy their jewelry so their families can eat. But, instead of going back to making illegal alcohol, they have chosen to trust God.

After repeating a grade level, Yo-Yo is now in the second grade. He is a leader in his class. Discussion groups are where he shines. When the groups share what they have learned, Yo-Yo is the first to volunteer.

He has learned to speak and read English well. He also ends up in the Principal's office regularly because he acts up in class. He is still learning to be patient and wait for instructions. He cares about doing well at school but finds it hard to listen when the teachers are teaching.

The older students at school play soccer during recess.

Yo-Yo would seem too young to play with the more former students, but jumps right in and is usually one of the team leaders.

We at Hope of the Nations know that God has big plans for Angel (Yo-Yo). He wants to be a pilot when he grows up, where he will fly around the world, reaching for the stars.

PATIENCE
Discussion Questions

1. What was Yo-Yo's real name? Do you have a nickname?

2. Are there times you have gotten in trouble at school? How could you have made better choices?

3. Are you a leader at school, like Yo-Yo? What sports do you like to play?

4. Read again about Yo-Yo's mother's patience. Do you think you could be patient like her?

5. How can you show patience to a family member, friend, or classmate?

6. What kind of patience will Yo-Yo need when he grows up?

7. Share times you have been patient, and times you have not shown patience. How did it feel? What happened?

Look in your downloaded folder for your FREE patience journal page.

JOYFULNESS

And do not be grieved, for the joy of the Lord is   your strength.

Nehemiah 8:10b

Joy is a sweet little girl who loves to sing songs to Jesus.

I first met Joy when she was only two years old. Her mother had visited a women's Bible study that I was teaching, and she brought Joy with her. During the Bible study, Paulina, her mother, asked me if she were to give her life to Christ, how would they live? Her current lifestyle was not one that was bringing glory to God. What does a person say to that? After much discussion about trusting God, Paulina prayed for forgiveness. She decided to trust Jesus with her life and the lives of her three children.

The next week, Paulina was in a life-threatening car accident. With no doctors in Kamala village to help her, she went home to stay in bed for the rest of her life. She was unable even to raise her head without help. Joy would grow up with her five-year-old brother and seven-year-old sister. All three children have different fathers. None of which took an interest in the children's lives.

There were no other family members to help little Joy.

Hope of the Nations decided to help by having a nurse from the USA come out and work daily with Paulina. Mama's Bible study brought food for Joy and her siblings. The family loved singing songs of praise to Jesus! Joy would sit at the end of her mommy's bed and sing to her. Kids Club leaders had taught Joy many different worship songs.

Every day, Nurse Joanna would do physical therapy with Paulina. Every day, many people from all over the world prayed that she would one day walk again. After backbreaking work, Paulina went from being able to sit up, to using a walker and then walking on her own. During this time, Joy never left her mommy's side.

In the five years since then, Joy has passed her fourth-grade National exams. Sadly Joy's mother passed away. She died of an HIV infection. We know we will see her again in Heaven. This turn of events has left Joy alone at home; her siblings are old enough to care for themselves. She needed to find a family to live with that would allow her to continue her education at our school. Several people wanted to take Joy into their homes to work as a house girl. If she did that, she would never get to finish school.

There are many children in Kamala village with the same issues as Joy and her siblings. A family from out of town decided to take Joy into their home. They promised to get her to school every day. After a few months, they found that it was impossible to keep this promise.

As of today, Joy lives with her older sister in Kamala village. She is doing well in school and sings in the school choir. I often think of her and her mother singing praise songs while she watched her mommy lie in bed all day.

Joy sings with Joyfulness to Jesus even during times of uncertainty. When Joy grows up, she wants to be a singer. She has said, "One day, I will make a CD with songs of praises to Jesus for my life."

JOYFULNESS
Discussion Questions

1. What brings you joy?

2. Do you think you could have joy if you had Joy's life?

3. What takes your joy away?

4. What did you learn about joy from Joy's story?

5. Helping others can bring joy. Is there a person in your life that is like Paulina that you can help?

6. Ask God how you can help someone else. Take steps to do so.

LOVE
Part 1

Beloved, let us love one another, for love is from God, and whoever loves has been born of God and knows God. Anyone who does not love does not know God because God is love.

I John 4:7-8

Ester is quiet, shy, and loves to learn.

Ester, her little brother, and her father came to Hope of the Nations Primary School looking for help. Ester had tangled hair and wore a torn shirt and skirt, but she had a sweet smile. Never would I know her mother had passed away three days before from a disease called malaria. It is common, even expected, to not show emotions when something terrible happens. Ester's father loved his children. He left his village to come to Kamala, where he might be able to better provide for Ester and her brother. It wasn't long before he found a field to farm.

Ester was six years old. She had never been to school or even seen a school. It was difficult for Ester to speak, and she had no idea how to hold a pencil or seen a coloring book. The village her family came from was remote with no schools or medical care.

That day we enrolled her in a Kindergarten class at Hope of the Nations Primary School. The school was scary for her. Everything was new. It took a few weeks to teach her how to use a pencil and crayons. She started to thrive under the loving care of her teachers.

It turns out that Ester had to repeat Kindergarten, but is now in fifth grade. In fourth grade, when she took the National exams. Ester passed with an eighty percent.! She plays jacks and swings with friends at school. After each school day, Ester lovingly takes care of her little brother and makes dinner for the family.

Her brother Lenny also attends Hope of the Nations Primary School. He knows how to write and can name all the primary colors. Ester has been a big help in his education. Happily, she can pass her classes as well.

Her father is doing well too. He has helped put in a garden at Hope of the Nations Primary School, which provides different foods for the school and families in the community.

When Ester grows up, she wants to be a nurse. Thinking of her mother, she wants to help people who get sick from diseases like malaria.

LOVE
Part 2

Beloved, if God so loved us, we also ought to love one another.
I John 4:11

John is a strong, intelligent, and bold boy.

John's older 'brother,' Derrick, came by the school to see if there was any room for his five-year-old 'brother,' John. School had already started, but somehow I knew God wanted this little boy studying with us.

His parents had both died in a village outside Kamala. Orphaned children are typically taken care of by the neighbors. They become your brother, sister, aunt, and uncle, even though they are not related.

At the age of five, John traveled by himself to Kamala, searching for a place to live. That's when Derrick found him.

Derrick explained to me how he had taken John into his home, but he had no money to pay for public school. I could not say no to this little boy that had come all this way. I felt as if God led John to us.

Derrick, a young single guy, loved John enough to take him into his home. Hope of the Nations needed to partner with Derrick in caring for John.

Even though the school had been in session for two months, John caught up quickly. He enjoyed every subject, especially those where he got the opportunity to build things.

His strong personality sometimes got the best of him. Like the time he was in seventh grade. John lifted the front end of my car! He was trying to help get my car out of the mud.

Now John has graduated from Hope of the Nations Primary School. He is a top student in his class and loves to work with his hands. Chemistry and Math are his favorite subjects. His secondary teachers can't believe how fast he is learning advanced science classes.

When John grows up, he wants to be an engineer or a taxi driver. His brother, Derrick, drives taxis, and John wants to be like him. God knows and has more plans for John. Because of Derrick's love for John, both have now experienced the love of Jesus. They both are believers in Jesus as their Lord.

That is real love.

As of 2020, John and Ester have graduated from Hope of the Nations Primary School. They are taking a stand for Jesus at their high school. John and Ester bring their Bibles to school and have started a Bible Study on campus. They both are kind and loving towards everyone.

LOVE
Discussion Questions

1. What do John and Ester have in common?

2. How did Derrick show love to John?

3. How much does God love John? Explain how God protected John. How much does God love you?

4. Why was Ester so scared at school? Have you ever felt alone and scared at school?

5. How did Ester's father show love to her and the school?

6. Life is hard in Kamala village. How do people show love to each other? How do you show love to your friends and family?

7. Do you know Jesus loves you? How do you know that?

8. Ask God how you can love others in your life. Write down your ideas in your journal. Share them with your family.

Pick one person in your life to share love uniquely.
Look in your downloaded folder for your individual
friendship cards.

THANKFULNESS

Thanks be to God for His inexpressible gift.

2 Corinthians 9:15

Jenny is a fun-loving, strong-willed little girl who loves to read.

Jenny has no siblings, and her only family is her mommy. They call her mama Jenny. There has never been a father in her home. In Tanzania, mothers always take the name of their first-born child as their name.

I met Mama Jenny when I first started a bible study in Kamala many years ago. During Bible study, I discovered that neither Mama Jenny nor Jenny knew how to read or write. It is a typical problem in Kamala village. The women usually need their daughters to stay home and help while they go to work in the fields.

When Jenny turned five years old, she started school at Hope of the Nations Primary School. That is when Jenny learned how to read, write and understand mathematics.

Most families do not have the money to send their children to school. Hope of the Nations has a free tuition program. For families in these situations they can work at the school instead. Working ensures that parents are part of the school community and not given a handout. Jenny's mommy helps by cleaning classrooms after school or sweeping the school play yard.

One day, while Mama Jenny was cleaning a classroom, I happened to walk by the room. I noticed she was holding a book to her chest, and tears were running down her cheeks. I was not sure if I should say something or walk on by and leave her alone. As I entered the classroom, she jumped and put the book down. She picked up her mop and continued cleaning. Being curious, I wanted to know what was so special about that book. When I asked her what she said surprised me. "I can't believe my little girl knows how to read. Jenny is the only one in my family who knows how to read and write. "I was looking at the book. I wasn't going to steal it." I could see she was not stealing. Reassuring her that I trusted her to clean and not take books, she went on mopping. As I was leaving the classroom, Mama Jenny ran up to me and gave me a big hug. She thanked me again and again for letting her child come to school.

I reminded her, saying, "Asante Sana Yesu," which means thank you, Jesus. After all, Hope of the Nations is Jesus' school, not mine. Then she said, "Asante Sana, Yesu!" Thank you, Jesus!

In the classroom, Jenny struggles and has repeated third grade. Our school's standards are high compared to other schools in Tanzania. Students have to receive seventy percent in all eleven subjects to be able to move on to the next grade. Jenny works hard in class and has a thankful attitude. She loves reading, especially on the Leap Pad computers. Jenny is part of the after school program.

Many other students love to stay and do their homework at school. Most days, I have to remind them to go home. School is their favorite place to be.

On the weekends, there are reading classes provided for adults. Mama Jenny has completed the first class. She now reads Swahili with her daughter and makes jewelry to sell. They use the money to buy food.

When Jenny grows up, she wants to be a teacher so she can teach others to read and write.

THANKFULNESS
Discussion Questions

1. What do people call Jenny's mom? Why?

2. What would your mom or dad's name be if you lived in Tanzania?

3. How do you think Jenny felt when she learned to read and write?

4. What does Jenny want to be when she grows up?

5. Why do you think Jenny never gave up?

6. Asante Sana Yesu. What does that mean? Why would we say that?

7. Share with your family what you are thankful for in school. What can you do to be grateful? Share with your family if you need to change an attitude about school.

In your downloaded folder you'll find FREE fun
bookmarks and cards.
Today's free pages include some fun Swahili words
you can learn and surprise your friends.

PEACE

For whoever desires to love life, and see good days, let him keep his tongue from evil, and his lips from speaking deceit:

Let him turn away from evil, and do good; let him seek peace, and pursue it.

1 Peter 3:10–11

Sarah loves Jesus as her Heavenly Father. She knows He will never leave her.

As Sarah's father loaded all the family's belonging into his truck, Sarah watched him move out of their little mud hut. He was leaving with everything. Sarah and her mother were being left behind. All the neighbors were glad to see him go. His yelling and screaming at Sarah would finally stop. Sarah's mommy was not home that day. She was cooking at Hope of the Nations Primary School. She had no idea that she would be coming home to an empty house and a tearful four-year-old Sarah.

A year later, Sarah entered Kindergarten. Her teachers said she was a joy to have in class, but she did not listen very well. She seemed to be restless. Most days, Sarah got in trouble for talking in class.

Now Sarah is in the first grade. Mr. Gombe is her teacher. He has helped Sarah to find peace with her father here on earth and Father in Heaven. Once Sarah heard about Jesus as her Father and understood that He would never leave her, or yell at her, she found peace. Sarah prayed and asked Jesus into her life. She believes Jesus is the Son of God and that He came to die for her sins. She knows Jesus is alive and she can talk to Him anytime. Sarah is now a child of God. The anger and restlessness that she had inside was causing her to disrespect her teacher in class. Disrespect is a sin. When she confessed with her mouth and believed in her heart that Jesus saves, peace came. She no longer wanted to talk out of turn in class or talk back to her teacher.

In her first grade class she is learning how to use her own chalkboard. Writing her name and doing simple math problems is fun with her very own chalkboard and chalk. All the students love to learn this way. Every student receives a new board when they start school.

Sarah also loves to play with play dough, pretend cooking toys, and puzzles. Each classroom has a large chalkboard painted on the wall. Writing exercise books, pencils and crayons are the supplies the students use. They also learn using manipulative math cubes. Even though Kamala village is the poorest village in Tanzania, our students receive the best education.

When Sarah grows up, she wants to be a cook like her mommy. She never sees her daddy anymore, but is at peace with that, and she talks with her Heavenly Father everyday.

PEACE
Discussion Questions

1. In the beginning of Sarah's story she had no peace. How can you tell?

2. What did Mr. Gombe teach Sarah?

3. What kind of peace can no one take away from you?

4. Anger can lead to sin. How do you feel when you are angry? What would be a more peaceful choice?

5. God can bring peace in your heart today if you ask Him. Do you have peace in your heart? Do you have peace with God as your Heavenly Father like Sarah?

6. What would peace look like in your life? Maybe you can draw a picture to show peace, share a story or look up in the dictionary the meaning of peace.

Look for your FREE Letter to God journal page in your download file.

ACCEPTANCE

See what great love the Father has lavished on us, that we should be called children of God! And that is what we are!

I John 3:1a

For I know the plans I have for you, declares the Lord, plans to prosper you and not to harm you, plans to give you hope and a future.

Jeremiah 29:11

Adam is a tall, quiet, and reserved boy who loves to draw.

When Adam was four years old, his family moved to Kigoma, Tanzania. His father accepted a job with Hope of the Nations. Kigoma is a large town right next to Kamala village. Adam, being the youngest of four children, didn't think much about the move.

Adam turned five shortly after their move to Kigoma. He started Kindergarten at Hope of the Nations Primary School. His class was full of very active children, most of whom were orphans. Adam never seemed to fit in. He was afraid of trying anything new. Some days Adam would sit at his desk and cry for his mother. Even though he was the same age as all the other students, he was much taller than anyone else in the class.

By the time Adam entered third grade, he was as tall as some of the sixth graders. People always thought he was in secondary school, but actually, he was only eight years old

The other students in his class had activities and studies they were enjoying, but not Adam. He still was afraid to try anything new. When the students went out to play soccer on the field, he would sit and watch. When the class had oral reports to give, he would speak so softly that no one could hear him. Teachers and staff met with Adam and his parents weekly, but his behavior stayed the same. How could we help him open up? What was going on inside his mind?

One day a group of boys from the fifth-grade class got into a fight. They were pushing and shoving one another. Somehow Adam got in the way of one of the blows. He fell to the ground, but he did not stay down. Surprisingly, Adam jumped up and started screaming at everyone. He did have a voice! With frustration, Adam said, "I never hit anyone before. Stop it!" The crowd stood in amazement.

Blood dripped from Adam's nose. He wiped away his tears and marched off to the office with the other boys.

Listening to the boys argue about who caused the fight. I noticed

Adam was sitting in the chair, struggling to hold back his tears. When it was his turn to share what happened, he cried out, "I'm sorry for not being like the rest of you. I'm sorry for screaming, for being tall, for not speaking out," and the list went on.

With this opening up, we could now help Adam. We could help him to accept himself as a child of God. For the next few months, we met with Adam to talk about how he felt and what he was thinking. When Adam had moved to Kigoma, he had left his tribe and some family members. Even though he was only four years old, it was a loss and still made him feel sad. In his tribe, all the people are very tall and quiet. They also keep cows for a living. Herding cows is not something you see in Kamala village. Many things about Kamala village are different than where Adam was born.

Adam is now in the sixth grade. He has learned to talk about what he is thinking. Drawing pictures of his life in Kigoma is a favorite pastime for Adam. He still is much taller than all his classmates, but he knows that God made him and that God has a purpose for his life.

When Adam grows up, he wants to be an artist and draw pictures of Africa for children's books. He also would like to translate at Hope of the Nations Bible College like his father.

Feeling different can make a person feel afraid and sad sometimes. But God makes us all unique. We are different; the tribes or places we come from are different and how we look and think. God knows each of us personally. He knows how many hairs are on our heads; he even knows what we think about, and he loves us. God gives everyone talents and abilities.

Adam graduated from Hope of the Nations Primary School. He passed the National exams and is now attending a private high school out of town. Adam has learned to share his feelings and open up to people. He leads the Christian club on campus. He also received a Student Leadership award from his teachers.

God is using Adam in amazing ways!

ACCEPTANCE
Discussion Questions

1. Have you ever had to move to a new place where everything is different? How did you feel?

2. Do you and Adam have anything in common? Or are you more like the other children in his class? How?

3. Are there times you wish you could speak out what you are thinking? What would you say?

4. Accepting yourself is important. Write down your top three strengths. Share them with others in your family. How has God made you different from those around you? How has he made you similar to those around you?

5. Write down your top two weaknesses. Share what you wrote with others in your family. How has God used your weaknesses to make you stronger?

6. Knowing who you are in Christ is the first step in accepting yourself. Christ thinks you are wonderful. He loves you no matter what your strengths or weaknesses are. How does that make you feel?

GRACE

There is no condemnation for those who are in Christ Jesus.
For the law of the spirit of life has set you free in Christ Jesus
from the law of sin and death.

Romans 8:1-2

Angel is a brave girl with a big voice and a little body.

When Angel first came to live with her grandmother, she was an infant. Angel was born in Dar Es Salaam, a big city, one thousand miles across the country from Kamala. Her parents chose to take Angel to the village so they could have careers in the big city.

Every summer, Hope of the Nations Kids Club leaders put on a camp for the Kids Clubs and students from the school. Visitors from the USA and Canada come to Tanzania and bring supplies to help put on these camps. It is an exciting time. The students wait all year long to go to the Kids Club Camp. Yet, there are over one thousand children who attend Clubs. Selecting children is a difficult job for the staff. Attendance and memory work are deciding factors.

When Angel was in 4th grade, she was one of the students selected to go to Kids Club Camp.

She had been attending the weekly Kids clubs and had

completed her memory verses as assigned. She also worked hard on controlling her tongue. Angel had struggled with being bossy throughout the school year. Now was her time to attend camp; she danced home with the precious permission slip in her hand. What she didn't know was that this was not going to make her grandmother happy.

Angel's daily after school routine consisted of a bath, nap, and homework. After homework, she was to eat dinner and go to bed. There was no time for playing or sharing about the day. Her grandmother thought playing was a waste of time. She felt that Angel needed rest, food, and to study hard if she was going to earn her way to a good education. If at anytime Angel did not perform in her studies, grandmother would beat her. Kids Club day was the only day that Angel's routine changed.

For some reason, her grandmother allowed Angel to attend the club, but only with a promise of doing extra schoolwork on Saturday.

On the day that Angel brought home her permission slip; she had hopes that grandmother would sign it. The signed sheet would mean a week of camp with her friends. No homework or naps and no grandmother to tell her she was not good enough. Freedom for one week! Her grandmother read the form and then tossed it aside. It was as if it wasn't real to her.

Angel was afraid to ask, but with a trembling voice, she

begged, "Can I please, grandmother, go to camp? I will be a good girl."

Her grandmother looked up at Angel and said with a bold voice, "NO! You have not been good enough, and you need to study harder, not play."

What had happened? Angel couldn't believe what she was hearing. Angel had done everything her grandmother had asked her to do. Over the past few months, she had not gotten in trouble at school, and she had worked hard to be kind instead of bossy. How could she not get to go to the Kids Club Camp?

The next day Angel came into my office with the unsigned permission slip. I asked why it wasn't signed. Angel explained that her grandmother had said no. I knew there had to be more to the story. I set out to go and meet with Angel's grandmother in hopes of convincing her to sign the permission slip.

Angel's grandmother and I sat in her living room on expensive over-stuffed couches. The furniture looked new. Everything in the place was dust free and resembled a shop instead of a home. Angel was not allowed to be in the room while her grandmother and I visited. We drank tea and complimented each other on our different customs. Because I came with a plan in mind, I was eager to get on with the subject of allowing Angel to attend camp. It is rude to start asking questions. In most of Africa, greetings and visits are very important. Usually, I enjoy the customs of Tanzania, but that day I was anxious to get to the point. Angels' grades were far above average. The permission slip had the daily schedule typed on it. There would be Bible memory, songs, dramas, crafts, and even swimming.

She asked me how long the playtime was? And would Angel be in bed by a specific time? Most of all, she didn't think that Angel could behave well enough. Her concern was that Angel would be a bad girl, and then what would happen?

I cringed, the conversation changed from camp to grace. This woman proclaimed to know Jesus Christ as her Savior. Yet, I found it hard to believe she had ever heard teachings on grace.

I reminded her of Romans 8:1-2: "For there is now no condemnation for those who are in Christ Jesus." For it is by grace, we are saved, not works." Angel's grandmother shared how she believed Jesus as the Son of God. She knew Jesus died for her sins, rose again, and is alive. What she couldn't believe was Jesus did all the work on the cross and that it was FREE. I explained how none of us are good enough, but when we have Jesus as our Savior, His blood covers all our sins. I called Angel into the room. Her grandmother said that all I had shared about grace was new information to her. Sadly, she restated that Angel still could not go to the Kids Club Camp. Angel sat on the floor at our feet and said she was sorry for not being a good girl. I knew if I stayed any longer

I would say something that would make things worse. I left to go home and pray.

Angel visited my office, where I shared the love of Jesus and more about grace with her. Angel prayed and asked Jesus into her heart. She told me it felt like an enormous mud-brick left her heart when she prayed to repent of her sins. Angel learned she does not have to work to receive love from Jesus. He loves her, and the work He did on the cross makes her a good girl. She doesn't have to worry about being good enough to please Jesus. He is already happy with her.

The next year Angel's grandmother did sign her permission slip! And Angel did get to attend camp for the first time.

Angel's grandmother still doesn't quite understand grace. She is still trying to earn her way to heaven. Unfortunately, Angel's parents never come and visit her. Even so, Angel knows her heavenly Father loves and cares for her. When Angel grows up, she wants to be a School Manager and have a place where children learn that Jesus loves them, and His grace is enough.

GRACE
Discussion Questions

1. Have you ever wanted to go somewhere or get something, but the answer was no? How did you feel? Why do you think the answer was no?

2. Angel struggled with being bossy to others. Share one of your struggles.

3. Grace- what does that mean? Read the dictionary definition. Then read what the Bible says Romans 3:23,6:23, and Romans 3:23.

4. What happens when we try to work for our salvation?

5. Jesus died on the cross and rose again. Do you believe that was enough to forgive all your sins? Even past sins? How about the ones you do now or in the future? Discuss this and then pray and ask God to help you understand grace.

6. If you have never prayed to ask Jesus to forgive your sins and come into your heart, now is a good time. You can talk to Jesus about anything. He is listening. Jesus loves you completely.

Look in your downloaded folder. There will be a
FREE GIFT waiting for you.

ABOUT THE AUTHOR

My journey to Africa started in 1975. At eight-teen years of age, I married the love of my life.

We served together in churches and Youth Camps. Even with great success, I longed to be on a foreign mission field.

After twenty-five years of praying to serve overseas, the time came.

In 2003 we moved to Denmark for training to open a YWAM Center in Tanzania, East Africa.

Leaving our three grown children was stressful and exciting all in one.

Then, there were no grandchildren, and now we have eight! They are my best critics.

God opened up doors for us to pioneer several different areas of ministry. From starting the first English Medium Primary School to putting a boat on the longest lake in the world! Other areas of ministry are H of N Bible College, Micro Business Center, and Youth Camps. This was NOT what either my husband or I expected.

It has been an AMAZING journey.

The two hundred plus students at the primary school have stolen my heart. Seeing them learn to read their Bible is very rewarding. Watching them grow up as leaders in their communities is a miracle.

I pray the stories in "When I Grow Up" opens your hearts to these precious children. These are the kids; many people told me not to waste my time educating. Well, we proved them wrong.

Hope of the Nations Primary School scored number 1 the last three years on their National Exams.

I am proud to say after ten years of pioneering the school, it now runs entirely by Nationals.

In HIM, Coni

ABOUT HOPE OF THE NATIONS MINISTRIES

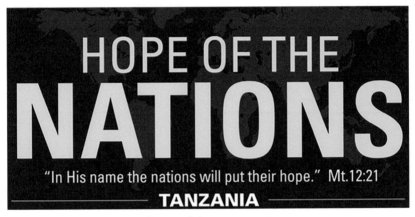

www.hopeofthenationstz.org

All proceeds from When I Grow Up go to support the children at Hope of the Nations Primary School in Kamala, Tanzania.

You are welcome to come and visit Tanzania. You and your family can meet the children from the book When I Grow Up. It is an exciting trip! Every year Hope of the Nations has visitors from all over the world come and see what God is doing.

For more information on how you can come out and serve, contact knepperstz@gmail.com or coniknepper@gmail.com.

Becoming a partner is an easy and fun way for the family to get involved in missions. Your monthly partnership of $35 provides:

- Bibles,
- two hot meals a day,
- uniforms/shoes,
- school supplies/books, and
- medical needs for students.

Send tax-deductible donations to this address:
Hope of the Nations
PO Box 1777
Woodbridge, CA 95258

Or give through our website: www.hopeofthenationstz.org

Prayer partners are always appreciated.

Contact Coni Knepper to receive monthly news updates at coniknepper@gmail.com. Also follow us on Facebook and Instagram.

Thank you for taking the time to read *When I Grow Up*. I pray it has been an adventure for you and your entire family.